Copyright © Yaffa AS

Published in 2023 by Meraj Publishing
Illustrations copyright © 2023
All rights reserved.

This is a work of creative nonfiction. Some parts have been fictionalized in varying degrees, for various purposes.

No part of this book may be reproduced or used in any manner without written permission of the copyright owner except for the use of quotations in a book review. For more information, address: info@merajpublishing.com

First paperback edition November 2023
Book design by Michael Colgan, Yaffa AS & Andrea Ramos Campos

merajpublishing.com

Blood Orange

By Yaffa AS

To those who dream of better worlds and those who build them.

Diaspora	8
I Am	9
Mother Tongue	11
Falasteen	13
On Our Way	15
Southwest	18
I Understand	20
Blood Orange	22
Cis white zionist	24
One Genocide	26
Healthy	27
At Odds	29
Tallying	31
When the World Ends	32
Lines and Circle	34
Every Fiber	36
Standing	37
Trans and Palestine	39
Relinquish	40
Questions in the Desert during an Eclipse	41
Resist	43
Stars	45
Count	46
Humanity	47
Mars	48
Whiteness Feeds	50
Marginalized	51
Amal	52
Victory	53

Tasleem   54
Ring of Power   56
Moving Piece   57
Land back   58

Diaspora

being in the diaspora
is having genocide
at your door
and you're not home to greet it

being in the diaspora
is wondering
which cut from your paycheck
killed your cousin

being in the diaspora
is being told
you are not from anywhere
while they kill you everywhere

being in the diaspora
is being
murdered
without ever bleeding

I Am

i am not
a body
you can murder

i am
a movement
you can't quench

i am not
a thought
you can extinguish

i am
a spark
you can't dim

i am not
an act
you can retaliate against

i am
a voice
you can't dull

i am not

a Palestine
you can erase

i am
indigenous sovereignty
you can't wipe out

i am
Palestine
indigenously sovereign
a movement
a thought
a voice
i am inevitable

Mother Tongue

they call it
mother tongue
because it is
meant to be
etched into
your being
because we all
have a
mother

so,
where do
the motherless
go?

those of us
without
a language to
ground us
a language to
remember us
remember me
when i don't
remember it
remember her

my mother
the mother of
my tongue
my people

i have a tongue
i have languages
and i have lost
my mother
tongue

because memory
and displacement
and dissociation
and learning
and unlearning
demanded her
loss

my loss

Falasteen

there are no
days without
Palestine in a heart
that was told
it was wrong
to yearn for
something that
was supposedly never
mine

my heart
yearns beyond
knowledge of what
was and will be
a certainty
words can never
define

i gaze
my third eye
stretching to fields
of citrus and olive
where blood is spilled
that feels and looks
like mine

mapping a trail
along nine countries
where blood and tears
store pieces of
indigeneity
that is mine

i wonder
when she will
call me home
opening her bosom
to states of awareness
beyond time
and place

i am and am not
home
for i am
Palestine and
she yearns for
me to taste
home

On Our Way

our bodies polarize
yet make the news
i am conscious
that other bodies
do not
a privilege is a privilege
even when it starts
and ends in genocide

our bodies are powerful
yet lie underneath tons
of concrete and rubble
that smells of jasmine
and sage, glazed in orange
and fig
drizzled in olive
oil that described Allah
in a lantern beyond

our minds warp
under the weight of
injustice in spilled blood
gaslighting and erasure
the weight of
indigenous genocide

fastened to our belts
released only when
we are

our people
rise like wisps
of rose water
breathing life
into knafe and
pistachio ice cream
on streets inscribed
in memories lost
to time fertilizing
homes we will
return to before
time begins

we are the beginning
and the end in a story
neither and yet
both at the same time

we are Palestine
call us by any other
name and we still are
what we are
Palestinians

Palestine
indigenous folks
on our way

Southwest

i don't know
if you're okay
names and faces
from years ago
family displaced
southwest rather than
southeast
lost at sea
in an open air prison
i may never see

i'm not sure
who to ask about
you, siblings to a
grandfather lost
to pandemics and time
children barely
remembering him
let alone you

do you remember
me like i remember
bits of you?
or am i lost
to memory

names and faces
that barely resemble
your Blackness
anymore
maybe you wonder
and say whatever
happened to those
who went southwest
instead of southeast?

I Understand

he said
you can't be
Palestinian
because you're
not white enough

they say
my people will
drag my
dead corpse
around

netenyahu
says we
caused the
holocaust

she refuses
to look my
way, stating
again and again
there is no
such thing
as a
palestinian

he says
i should beat
you to a pulp
but why do what
trains can

i understand

i understand

Blood Orange

i am of
a people who
have died a
thousand times
as white people
came and conquered

our blood filling
trees and canyons
turning the
sea a blood orange
like an eclipse that
forgot to
subside

the world ends
anew here
again and again
we are the
final test
of a humanity
that continues to
fail

angels watch

bathing in lot's sea
wondering why
you have been
permitted to
continue on
again and again

time ends
life begins
still we are

still we will
be your
envy and hate
your terror in
a night you
created for
yourself

Cis white zionist

he says
you're still welcome
here
we love you

as if my
people's genocide
that he upholds
supports
pays for
is not cause
to stay away
as if all
their lives mean
nothing compared
to a single
relationship forced
upon me
in the first place

he doesn't
know or understand
that even if
i loved him most
he is nothing

compared to every
indigenous person
out there

the caucasity
of cis-white zionists
to believe they
matter more
than the world

One Genocide

is it all
only one
genocide
if they
can't tell us
apart across
hundreds of years?

Healthy

we are
not meant to
be okay when
genocide is
our neighbor
that is funded
by our labor

we are
meant to be
a mess
our sleep
tearing into
reality
anxiety brewing
wondering what
is hope?

we are
meant to
tear at the seams
of reality
realizing a reality
built on oppression
is bullshit

we are
meant to
realize and demand
all we are worth
self-actualization
wholeness
things systems
built off of genocide
can never

our response
labeled by
western capitalism
as wrong is
healthy
we move to
wholeness
always
they move to
pain, attempting
to drag us
with them

At Odds

my transness and
a colonized perception
of Palestine are at
odds

they think it's
because of islam
lack of modernity
i say i have only
received death threats
targeting my
transness from
white people, zionists
and other
various political
affiliations

i say only yt
people around me
have ever disowned
their own
yet i do not
talk to sisters
who choose to buy
into imperialist transphobia

claiming it as
their own

my parents
do not understand
how some of
their children
could hate anything
any of their
children could be
why anyone
would hate what
they do not
know

Tallying

i make a
list, tallying
who says what
when, where
or who does not
say what
when, where
crystallizing
support and
hypocrites
who ultimately
build a world
not made for
us

When the World Ends

i tense
at nightmares
awake
my sleep filled
with rest
the touch of
another so
far from my
truth

your singing bowls
calm an ocean
of catastrophe
precipitating into a
hurricane off
every coast

thank you reiki
i am open to accepting
your hands glide
along my skin
my chakras awakening

you do not
understand

but understanding
has never been
necessary to
support

you stand by
arm there when
i need it
taking care of
someone who has
never learned to
accept care

when the world
ends
i know only you
will think of me
then

Lines and Circle

you drew a line
when you said
you didn't have
to tolerate queer
and trans people

you drew a line
when you said
a settler colonial
state is valid
in defending itself
leading to genocide

you drew a line
when you said
cops are necessary
to maintain
the peace

you drew a line
when you said
all lives matter
Black-on-Black crime
a few bad apples
as if the orchard

didn't need
torching

you drew a line
when you said
pro-life
it's a woman's choice
that this is unlivable
when rights have never
been ours

you drew a line
when you said
anyone blue
as if blue and red
are not siblings

you've drawn
every line
there could be
while we
wait for a circle

Every Fiber

if you count
every fiber
in a Yaffa orange
will you find
my dead people?
my family?
me?

Standing

"i stand with"
Palestine
Armenia
indigenous folks
everywhere
does not feel adequate

is it standing
when i have voted
for people who
killed my family?

is it standing
when i go to a single
protest while you
are carpet bombed
with phosphor?

is it standing
when i realized politics
is not made for
someone like me and
i am next?

is it standing

when i am a settler
my indigeneity murdered
thousands of miles away?

is standing
flying across oceans
allowing my body
to ricochet off
the sea
into utopia and
oblivion?

what is standing
if not ableist
jargon that pretends
that i'm doing
anything at all?

i stand
you die
until tomorrow
i die
you stand

Trans and Palestine

if I was not trans
would Palestine be free?
no, then how fucking
dare you bring it up
instead of saying
Free Palestine!

Relinquish

we know it ends
in flame because those
with power were never
taught to relinquish

we wait for them to
we forget you can't
give up what wasn't
yours to begin with

Questions in the Desert during an Eclipse

if i was assigned
female at birth
would i be able to
die in Palestine?

is there any
part of me
i can sacrifice
for a free
Palestine?

if i never
step in
Palestine
will Falasteen
remember
me at all?

if the moon
stopped
will Palestine be
free before
the next ice age?

if joy is
revolutionary
how much ecstasy
do i need
to free Palestine?

Resist

we do not
resist because
one action
will free us
today

we do not
resist for
a free
Palestine
today

we do not
resist for
more
privilege
today

we do not
resist for
a return to
peace
today

we resist

for a free
decolonized
world
today
tomorrow
every day

Stars

the stars
rest
at ease
safe away from
genocide and pain

i wonder if they
also look at us
and wonder
why we are
the way we are

a child stares
at the same stars
but theirs comes
to meet them
phosphor filling
their lungs

i envy them
returning
to stars
that don't
know

Count

if there's
no one
to count the
dead do they
not count?

Humanity

we have learned
again and again
no one will save us
yet still we try
we wait and wonder
if maybe this time
humanity wins
forgetting humanity
has not meant anything
for hundreds of years

Mars

i am befuddled
by a decolonized mars
it's funny that
we decolonize what has existed
billions of years before
colonization

if mars is the outsider
then is mars our planet?
if mars is everything white people
despise, then is mars a trans poc?
if mars is a symbol for the military,
is mars a response to us?

it feels like within an imperialist
world, mars is the planet of those
of us at the margins of marginalization

whiteness says mars is about
communication and sex
but communication is for the
civilized, the white
sex is for the innocent, also white

our communication is punished
used against us, daily and systemically

our sex is placed upon us
our bodies defiled
worthless to begin with

our bodies, our land, our resources
our being fetishized
existing only within whiteness
cannibalized
denying the red
of our blood

Whiteness Feeds

off of Black and brown
flesh, calling us the cannibals

whiteness feeds
off of Black and brown
culture, calling us the uncultured

whiteness feeds
off of Black and brown
land, calling us wasteful

whiteness feeds
off of Black and brown
souls, calling us disconnected

whiteness feeds
itself
cannibalizing nations in
armies, as tourists
as social workers in
war zones they create

whiteness wants to be
so much more
whiteness fails

Marginalized

to be marginalized
is to be weaponized
against others
on the margins
to maintain our
and their marginalization
we are weapons of
war against ourselves

Amal

there will come
a day when
the sun sets on
a world and rises
in another
where indigenous
sovereignty
is honored
where queerness
no longer
exists
where transness
is no longer
an identity
where humanity
means something
genuine

Victory

she stares back
showered in roses and applause
bow in hand
horse glorious
she is victory

victory is deceptive

do they determine victory
or
is victory victory
even when there are
no roses, no applause

when a child is
lost to rubble
are they also
victorious?
or is
victory in the hands who
pull the trigger?

Tasleem

how do you
un attach
when your people
   -   any people
are being butchered?

how do you
have faith
when genocide
is at your doorstep
and you are not home
to answer it?

how do you
surrender
when you never had
control
in the first place?

we surrender
because
we never had control
in the first place

we have faith

because our
unseen has been
our only
embrace

we un attach
because we are not
a mind and body
we are endless

Ring of Power

the moon and sun
part after
embracing
in a ring of fire

how many millions of factors
needed to align
to allow this celestial embrace?

if all of those could align
a free Palestine
seems so easy

Indigenous sovereignty
is guaranteed

Moving Piece

it is neither
the sun nor the moon
moving
that shows them
intersecting

it is the earth moving

settler colonial states
will always be
just that

indigenous folks
will always
resist

we are the moving piece

Land back

i do
not know names
wiped from
time in Gaza
like i do
not remember
the names of
great uncles and
aunts who
have been reclaimed
by our land

to say they
were murdered
is to claim loss
that our land
will never feel
for we are made
of her and
regardless of how
many layers of phosphor
fill the air
we return to
her in our deaths
they may

exacerbate the
process of our
return but return
we shall

standing thousands
of miles away
i know even here
she will take
me back
for distance
is a creation
that is buried
with bodies
that were never
ours

we are not
the ones who
take land
back
it is land
that takes us

Acknowledgements

I extend immense gratitude to every individual who has raised their voice against the ongoing genocide and who strive to create a world devoid of settler colonialism. A heartfelt thank you to Michael Colgan for his unwavering support— from editing and cover design to strategizing and so much more. I owe a special note of appreciation to Andrea Ramos Campos; without her strategic collaboration, this book might not have seen the light of day. Mama Ganuush, your continuous support in my daily life and during the in-person launch was invaluable. To Kanzi Kamel and Ave', thank you for your cherished friendship and unceasing support throughout this journey.

A deep thanks to George Ramirez, not only for his contributions to the cover design but also for being a steadfast pillar in my life, supporting me through what feels like multiple lifetimes.

To my parents and family members who have always seen and supported me in every facet of who I am, I owe you endless gratitude.

I'm grateful to Queer Arts Future and Moment Cooperative and Community Space for their relentless work in uplifting the queer and trans communities every day, and for their steadfast backing with the launch of "Blood Orange". My gratitude also extends to Hannah Moushabeck, Tori Lanett, Lamya H, and Shereen Sun for their insightful advance feedback. A nod to Eman Abdelhadi, who passionately envisions a free Palestine and undertakes incredible work towards that vision. And lastly, to anyone I may have inadvertently missed: it truly takes a community to breathe life into any work, and for that, I am eternally grateful.

About the Author

Mx. Yaffa is an acclaimed disabled, autistic, trans, queer, Muslim, and indigenous Palestinian individual who has received multiple awards for their transformative work around displacement, decolonization, equity, and centering the lived experiences of individuals most impacted by injustice.

Mx. Yaffa is the Executive Director of Muslim Alliance for Sexual and Gender Diversity (MASGD, as well as the founder of several non-profits and community projects.

Mx. Yaffa is an engineer, death and birthing doula, peer support specialist, consultant, and artist.

Mx. Yaffa is a storyteller and an equity and transformation consultant, having shared their story with over 150,000 audience members at speaking events globally.

About Meraj Publishing

Meraj Publishing is a Trans and Queer Muslim publishing house that centers TQM voices from the global majority. Recognizing the vast inequities in the publishing industry, we aim to enable TQM individuals from the global majority to fully own our stories. Meraj prioritizes stories that focus on building utopia, hope, love, spirituality, and belonging. Meraj Publishing is entirely run and operated by the TQM global majority.

Milton Keynes UK
Ingram Content Group UK Ltd.
UKHW021558071024
2051UKWH00071B/1618